Stream of Deer

STREAM OF DEER

Kamran Mir Hazar

Poetry

Translation:

Marta Núñez Pouzols

Nushin Arbabzadah

STREAM OF DEER

Kamran Mir Hazar

Poetry

Poems translated by Marta Núñez Pouzols are from *Choros De Ciervos translated by Manuel Llinás* and Rafael Patiño Góez.

Poems translated by Nushin Arbabzadah were published on the website of the Rotterdam Poetry Festival at www.poetryinternationalweb.net. Translation © 2010 by Nushin Arbabzadah.

Copyright © 2014 Kamran Mir Hazar
www.kamranmirhazar.com
All rights reserved.
ISBN: 978-0-9837708-5-5

Data code on the cover was taken from "Stuxnet Under the Microscope" by ESET.

Full Page Publishing
411 Walnut Street
Davidson, NC 28036 USA
www.FullPagePublishing.com

Robert Maier, Editor for Full Page Publishing

To my family

CONTENTS

1	STREAM OF DEER	Pg 1
2	PETREL	Pg 4
3	A STORY OF PHILOSOPHERS AND SAVAGES	Pg 8
4	REVIVAL OF A MEMORY OF NAZIM HIKMET	Pg 15
5	AHMAD AMIR ALAI	Pg 19
6	PICTURE	Pg 20
7	CREATION WORKSHOP	Pg 22
8	PAINTING	Pg 24
9	SHE BROUGHT EMOTION IN THE SHIRT FROM PAKTIKA	Pg 26
10	FROZEN TRAIN	Pg 28
11	MEXICO	Pg 30
12	THE CRY OF A MARE ABOUT TO BECOME A BUTTERFLY	Pg 32
13	A BRONZED FACE AND TINY PURPLE VEINS	Pg 38
14	VIRUS WRITING	Pg 44

STREAM OF DEER

While they are coming to fix the sound,
While they are coming to either cover up my breath
with shadows
Or to bring a mirror
For me to stand in front of,
Being 5 feet and 5 inches tall,
With my hair combed and my neck embroidered
with filigree.
And I see a train with its wide rails,
Speeding up my throat now
While they want to show me a man
Sitting behind a desk,
Adjusting a pair of glasses,
The wind bringing him his own dreams

Along with this stream of deer,

Along with this moment that I spend with Mir Hazar,

Along this riverbed,

Along this wind which has blown through women's bracelets,

Which has blown through doves' collars,

And has spilled over the mountain,

And has withered.

It has withered, and it has listened to the song of all the failed ones,

And it has set off to me

In this exhibition of paintings and calligraphies,

Towards these naked voices,

Which gather either in the extension of the deer's antler

Or in the precise moment in which the train and his eyes interweave,

Along with me, hurried from the train cars

When his motorcar stops,

When he walks

The last steps of his life

Very
Very
Slowly
And he stops by the exhibition
With a captivating light that lands in the bottom of the glass.

Someone arrives
And unplugs the TV set.

PETREL

From high descent,

Penetrating look,

The arousal of her eyebrows merged into the heat of the skin,

Perhaps wrapped in silk,

Perhaps in the seaman's dream

Or in the harmonious inner pace

Suspended in the clock hands of breath,

Or perhaps walking in a generous paradise of savages.

In that moment sacrificing oneself was unavoidable.

Shattered and bolting rebellion

In the color of the petrel's beak—

Or the moment in which her body was passed from hand to hand
And nobody knew that she had been shot,
But it was not the bullets that destroyed her.

Bolting rebellion in the color of the petrel's beak.

In that moment she was neither meek lamb nor furious panther;
She took a cigarette and lit it, in that moment,
And she started walking towards the sail of the boat,
And she took on a color in between olive and water,
And the melody returned to its beginning,
And the quivering and undulating composition was heard again,
Immediately mastering word and conventions,
And in that moment, in the subdued heat of a wind instrument, she took shape,
And in that moment she was an accomplished drunk,
And stumbling she mastered expression and time.
The melody returned to its beginning

And the quivering and undulating composition was heard again,
Again it flowed,
And from the woman's mouth it bloomed.
In a majestic hall a blue light bouncing back,
Making the memory of the young admiral bustle.
In that moment she was neither meek lamb nor furious panther;
She was prudish as a pregnant woman,
She did not feel like drinking wine,
And she had fled from the brothels,
And she spent that month lost in thought—
The sadness of the admiral who will drown in a river,
The jellyfish never danced with sorrow.

The light bounces back from the sand
And passes over her crystalline body.
It comes back
And yields to her eyelashes,
Those moments of lust will not come back.

She was prudish as a pregnant woman,
She was pregnant:
Her body swayed.

Bolting rebellion in the color of the petrel's beak.
With the harmonious inner pace a turmoil
Traverses the fishnet garment.
In that moment the tar ribbon was trespassed;
In that moment, she was neither meek lamb nor violent panther.

A STORY OF PHILOSOPHERS AND SAVAGES

one

Have you ever felt strange?

Something weird is happening on the screen:

A worn out dusk,

A worn out day.

Someone remembers you tonight

In the streets of the capital,

Someone remembers you tonight

Near the square,

Near the station,

In the room,

Near the books,

Have you ever felt strange?

The camera zooms on your empty seat,

The filmmaker is very unhappy.

two

Unhappy filmmaker,

Unhappy audience,

What are you doing?

Look at my saddened land:

The strong smell of the generals' armpits,

The law will be executed today

While anxiously calibrating their guns,

While the camera travels to an abandoned printing press.

three

Alice in wonderland,
Alice in my land.
Alice next to a flowering shrub,
In my city, sitting at the hustlers table
While the sallow light overflows on the cards;
Under the projection of a cactus' shadow
While men who live by dreaming of a sad woman
fight a duel.

This is the world,
Entirely a story of philosophers and savages.
This is the world,
In an abandoned printing press
A story of warriors in some place similar to Texas
Betting to be the one to touch a woman.

four

I know of your racing heartbeat because of a national anthem,
I know of your sorrow, too much sorrow to love,
But restrain yourself
When the beggars come and go.
Do not set your dogs on me,
Restrain yourself.
Days go by one after the other
Without leaving the chance to name anyone,
Days go by one after the other.
Love, wherever it comes from, drives one to insanity.

I have written your name over the mountains,
I have written your name next to the statue of Bamiyan Buddha,
I have written your name over the Mediterranean sea[1].

---

[1] Thank you, Paul Eluard.

Your name evaporates

And freedom spreads out through the world.

You are not done, not even in Siberia,

Where the sick ones call you with the steam of their breaths.

five

I pronounce this poem for Alice,
I address her thus for the first time,
Without knowing how much my Alice knows about
the story of Nazim Hikmet
Or whether she has even read the letters of Chaplin.

When Nazim addresses his lover
He talks of the revolution,
Of pins and shirts,
Of revolutionary flags.
My Alice must have read the letters of Chaplin,
Since she knows the weeping sound
Of a man who makes everyone laugh.
Strange is our world, Alice,
I still sing elegies for the loved ones.

REVIVAL OF A MEMORY OF NAZIM HIKMET

The rattling of the train makes everything crumble,

When I open the compartment door

A light stretches to the end,

It's tail bends over a woman's legs.

I come in,

I greet,

There is no answer,

There is no one.

I leave my backpack,

I take off my jacket,

I sit down,

There are several hours left until Izmir.

I fix my gaze upon her face,

It seems that she has closed her eyes.

Half of her hair falls down over her breasts,

A light comes and goes over her legs,

Pink pants

And blue shoes

In complete silence,

Inside the compartment there is complete silence,

Not interrupted even by the train.

Everything barely goes up and down,

Just like she goes up and down

And I myself go up and down.

The rattling opens the compartment door even more.

And now the light from the hall spreads all over her body:

Pale face,

Eyes shut down.

She sleeps,

It is really strange.

Have you ever read *Sleeping Beauty and the Airplane*?

It is so strange

And she is beautiful,

So beautiful,

Her legs joined together,

Her thin and translucent hands,

Her half-sleeved blouse,

Blue

English collar,

Pale face I said.

Eyelashes obscuring her closed eyes

As if sprinkled with kohl,

As if on her way to her lover.

Fine chin,

Her lips seem to be awaiting the kiss,

As if a lover were to arrive and take her in his arms.

I get up,

I go out,

The noise of the train makes everything crumple.

I walk down the corridor,
Outside blinking headlights like oil lamps.
I come back,
Her legs are repositioned,
Now her hair is tied back.
Oh my God she has woken up.
She greets,

I greet—
My hands warm.
She talks

And I do not understand even my own words,
But her lips drawing in and growing apart.
Oh my God
Ankara-Izmir is such a beautiful route.

AHMAD AMIR ALAI

His face,

His height,

Didn't even fit in the camera.

When he had fixed his tie

Everyone took their pictures,

And even when they brought in his corpse

Nothing could be done,

I was only a reporter.

PICTURE

one

Maybe it is afternoon

In the shade of an almond tree,

The particles they talk about are absent,

Sure it is cold in the mountains.

Look,

Look at the right side of the picture.

Is that a man with a Kalashnikov? What does that mean?

two

A prince by himself
With a pensive wrinkle as far as the gap in the temple.
What is it that shakes in your eyes?
I administer an oath to the prince
On behalf of the mountains,
On behalf of the simple people in his kingdom.
What do the prince's eyes truly express?

Look,
Something similar to an afternoon,
My father standing, by himself.
Look at the right side of the picture again.

CREATION WORKSHOP

That restless unity between her lips,
That beautiful architecture of the body,
Of expression and of the body,
And a fired up arch covering the upwards slope of her back.

Drink the wine at every moment?,
Because this flavor shall not be forgotten;
Drink the wine at every moment,
Because every moment is a treasure,
Every moment her eyebrows are in our poems,
Her look,
Her walk.

A big heart in the creation workshop,
Quiet expression between her fingers,
between the turning and the constant kisses
And again moving away.
Moving away up to the point

Of the station where we came to say goodbye to her.

PAINTING

one

I have closed my eyes,
I close them
To block my tears.

I want to flee the place where all the bullets aim,
The place where I fell martyr so many times.
I rose up,
I fell down again.
I want to flee all the paintings
And the jammed movement of the brushstrokes,
I want to flee the paintbrushes
And the tearful look, even of the woman who painted me.

two

All the anthems are sung for you,
All the chants,
And on the stage all the dances will be performed.
There is torment for every person
And dreams, for those you can use as hideouts.
The sea is for you,
And the look of sailors running
After a girl's body on the deck;
This vessel will approach Paris
For the Parisian writers to mention between stories
that sad girl;
This vessel will approach Paris,
It will approach the right corner of a painting in the
Louvre,
Where human suffering hides in paint,
Among hues of blue.

SHE BROUGHT EMOTION IN THE SHIRT FROM PAKTIKA

Sometimes, beside a vague poppy scent
Those aspects of passing are found.
He brought in the shirt from Paktika unreached emotion,
Not reached by any stranger.
Noon
Goes by,
The rural heat of the summer;
And do not ask the fatigued narrators whether the sultan with his steles,

His mountains,

His wind,

Will bring sadness from the dry instead of joy.

The narrator cannot tell anything

For himself in brackish drops,

The narrator...

He cannot!

No balm can heal my Kabul from its wounds.

FROZEN TRAIN

One layer trickles down to another
The tongue between the slip of two fragilities;
You hear how that slippery and simple layer
Mingles sometimes
with thick Urdu.
A little boy begins to speak in an urban train,
Sometimes Urdu and sometimes Norsk[2] with
something of Bergensk[3];
They overlap, they are greased every few levels,
They carry this frozen train towards Østerås[4]
As if tongues rubbed each other.
In Røa[5] someone brings his lighter closer to a piece of tin foil,

---

[2] Norsk or Norwegian: language from Norway.
[3] From Bergen, city in West Norway.
[4] Area in the outskirts of Oslo.

Takes the heroin out of its plastic wrapping

And answers the phone with a heavy accent from Bergen:

Det er fint vær

men det blir finere

unnskyld, jeg har dårlig batteri[6]

da snakkes vi.

---

[5] Neighborhood in Oslo.
[6] Translation: The weather is nice / but it is going to get even better / I'm sorry, I'm running out of battery / we'll talk later

MEXICO

poem for Juan Rulfo

Mexico:

Someone is committing suicide,

Someone is mending sacks under an October moon,

Someone has returned to Talpa de Allende.

Mexico:

Open the windows,

Someone is carrying a coffee tray,

Offering coffee cup by cup,

Someone has released the collar of his shirt,

Ready to pass through the river,

And someone must take our group's photograph on time.

Mexico:
The birds are dead.

Mexico:
Suicide with this knife is no longer possible.

Mexico:
Juan Rulfo the pitiful.

THE CRY OF A MARE ABOUT TO BECOME A BUTTERFLY

One

Continually over the water, horizon,

Split River,

Forked Oxus,

Someone is making a stand;

Or maybe

A Hindu spell over the sand,

Moving, wandering, over paths and landing at the foothills of words;

Each time to become speech, to connect or maybe disconnect;

A wet inkpot,

Curled inside the glass vessel,

Connecting itself just so to leave the self behind,
The coiled breath touches the rims of a clay cup,
The five senses become three dimensional,
Curling, uncurling, in the excitement of sealed lips,
A wandering person moves along a path, carrying the cancer;

Steamed breath resting on the teacup,
The stares roped together,
And the melancholy of sweet Chinese aromas;
A body-part of ours has left for Tibet,
The cry of a mare about to become a butterfly.

two

Cans of beer and a fistful of dollars,
He looks her down and up,
With his Mediterranean gaze,
Swaggering, he moves up the cannabis leaf,
Burning the gaze in the fire of words

August the third he packed his bags,
Setting off towards an illusion far away,
Way beyond civilization;

three

One said let's drink this cup of freedom,
One ran and ran along the corridor of electrons,
One entered the path,
One reached the bridge, the self becoming oneself,
The gods and laughter through the lips.
Are you there yet?
The place where the path is the path and the walker on the way;
When the shifting sands sharpen to become dunes,
moving on and bringing you

To the Nimrooz desert,
Malayalam is present;
A peculiar geometric composition.

four

And I couldn't carry on,

The self that I've been in the mountains;

Herding sheep,

Bent, carrying dead poppies on my back;

The lords of the land had already borne the fresh ones,

Yet the book found a new face,

The book became a clue to wisdom,

Opening doors so they are expanded,

five

Dressed in the garment of purity,
The snow-covered firs of Herat,
An attempt for town life to return,
So that I need not write anything;
The one, the swirling one,
Looking at nothing, unlike a self,
Has walked the distance; has shown forbearance;
A non-self, swirling on the most feverish of Kabul nights,

The weather was not cold,
But curled in a corner,
Snow was moving up those veins.

A BRONZED FACE AND TINY PURPLE VEINS

A bronzed face and tiny purple veins,
A smooth face of Mayan mold,
The colors of saffron and pasture,
Hunched in a bright overcoat
And woolen hat,
The long coat's tassels wary of the slashing winds of mountain land,
On the invisible flag: whiteness and the antlers of a stag
With a heart dispersed and diffused;
Ferried by a gramophone's sound waves,

Sensation is channeled in the air,

The command, the book and the empire of catapults, and way before

A sensation is in the air, expanding

In the arm, and the disintegrating arm,

In the solitude of darkness

And when someone's death is announced in the hour of divination,

Hiding from life,

And escaping between the clear and the blurred faces,

A desire for the pulse to drop,

In the cleft of a ruby; the fruit of Badakhshan ; and a crying face;

In the birth of eyelashes and the soft fabric of shivering dew,

To appear and to nestle between tresses,

The burning of intense fever, lubricious more than ever, magnetic more than ever;

Swinging in the direction of inopportunity, the wheel of fortune, turning

And standing;

In a curling clock destined to melt,
Slippery on the cheeks, the annihilator of the restless cloak, endlessly turning;
You stand,
You watch,
You drink tea;
Like a rainbow, you drop on the chair;
You pick up a cigarette,
And light it;

The flickering lantern awakens,
Swirls around the cloak,
Rising from the margins, colored blue,
And stands on your heart,
Evaporates through your eyes;
Creeping to a corner is an emerald ring stone,
The slippery past of a faraway destiny,
And you reach the curved line,
Entering a geography of latitudes and longitudes,

The composition quickens;
In the middle of the open field, again and again,
A church turns into ruins,
Recomposing in the breaking of light and the unique path of your voice,
And passes through latitudes and longitudes;
The heat lifts the cloak,
Settling on the crucifix of your ribcage,

On the chair, shivering,
With the fluttering fabric of dew
You drink tea,
You light up the rainbow lamp,
You drown,
And the pen turns round and round,
And you write your own death;
It moves up your fingers,
Pursuing the path to your mouth,
You collapse within your pulse,
You write this,
And you disintegrate between the seconds;

You go to the post office,

You ask for a letter of the perished,

Searching for an omen;

You take the by-way,

You look for an epiphany,

In a rainbow shawl,

And shake crimson-colored medals,

You say hello, peace be upon you,

And then goodbye;

You are dispersed between the sound waves of a gramophone,

Your heart diffused and ferried by the sound waves of a gramophone,

You stay at home

And seek prophecy,

Searching for an omen in the hours;

The bronzed face heats up,

You wrap yourself around my body;

Looking for where the breaths join up,

You're released in my throat;

You move up,

Become tears

And flow down my cheeks;

You go to the post office,

Seeking a letter from the dead;

A longing to let go,

A date with the unsung heroes of time,

And empires beyond the age when writing was invented;

The ones that were never put in ink,

Embarking on the saddle, taming the lines,

Abandoning time, leaving the five senses behind;

That bronzed face, a prototype found when iron was discovered

A one that never, ever found reflection in ink.

VIRUS WRITING

one

Writing viruses
And electronic labyrinths
With a blackout and no computer
In a rented house, at seven thousand a month;
Kabul, the Afghan capital!
What silly poem is this?

You ask yourself, is poetry the same lonely words
that wander in electronic corridors,
Cut off from their existence,
Thrown away, with no choice but to become a poem?

You watch imagination wandering through paths,
over the paths,
You throw the leash at yet another word,
Trying to subdue this wild one,
And if you fail,
You stop functioning,
Like a computer crashed.

two

There was someone, someone who wrote viruses
Behind a diesel-powered laptop
Looking for URLs and
An anonymous mail would be sent
Connecting you to a site, infected;
"I am from Florida, the USA, and 23 years of age,
Looking for someone to follow the link, and make happy";
To open the mail and to make someone happy?
First, stop the programs;
Passing through security, typing 97, 98, 99,
Approaching the death of romance between zero and one.

A virus-writer drank half a beer bottle at once;
Then, computer deaths;
First to the east of Paris, a house,
Australia, three minutes more,

A man is waiting out the last minutes of an office shift
Needs to get home;
A party is starting in half an hour;
The Philippines, minutes later,
A 19-year-old girl
in a chat room,
Showing off a used body;
In Egypt, more or less the same time,
And the next morning, Kabul.

three

You, and you, also you,
Yes, you and also you,
You are all arrested!

four

They tell me, stop writing!

You write and we'll show you Guantanamo at home,

You write, we'll kill you.

Kabul, summer of '07

Hands in handcuffs, feet tied up;

This is Afghanistan, and this here, where is it going,

Dead bodies over dead bodies.

The poem has no choice but to stop writing itself.

This is prison.

five

They asked a Kabul sparrow
Just what is mankind up to?
The sparrow considered this and died!

Poems translated by Marta Núñez Pouzols
- STREAM OF DEER
- PETREL
- A STORY
- OF PHILOSOPHERS AND SAVAGES
- REVIVAL OF A MEMORY OF NAZIM HIKMET
- AHMAD AMIR ALAI
- PICTURE
- CREATION WORKSHOP
- PAINTING
- SHE BROUGHT EMOTION IN THE SHIRT FROM PAKTIKA
- FROZEN TRAIN

Poems translated by Nushin Arbabzadah
- MEXICO
- THE CRY OF A MARE ABOUT TO BECOME A BUTTERFLY
- A BRONZED FACE AND TINY PURPLE VEINS
- VIRUS WRITING

Meet Kamran Mir Hazar

www.kamranmirhazar.com

kamran@kamranmirhazar.com

www.facebook.com/kamranpoetry

Spanish edition of Stream Of Deer

CHORRO DE CIERVOS

Kamran Mir Hazar

Poesía
Traducción:

Manuel Llinás

Rafael Patiño Góez

Primera Edición: 2012
Full Page Publishing
ISBN: 978-0-9837708-4-8

POEMS FOR THE HAZARA

An anthology and collaborative poem contributed by 120 poets from 66 countries

Executive editor Kamran Mir Hazar

Our poets represent world poetry today: Etnairis Ribera, Puerto Rico/ Angelina Llongueras, Catalonia/ Aju Mukhopadhyay, Pondicherry, India/ Ban'ya Natsuishi, Japan/ Julio Pavanetti, Uruguay/Spain/ Gertrude Fester, Rwanda and South Africa / Jack Hirschman, USA / Iztok Osojnik, Slovenia/ Erling Kittelsen, Norway/ Obediah Michael Smith, Bahamas/ Bina Sarkar Ellias, India/ Raúl Henao, Colombia/ Anne Waldman, USA/ Nguyen Quang Thieu, Vietnam/ Timo Berger, Germany/ Elsa Tió, Puerto Rico/ Kamran Mir Hazar, Hazaristan/ Rodrigo Verdugo, Chile/ Mildred Kiconco Barya, Uganda/ Stefaan Van Den Bremt, Flanders, Belgium/ Winston Morales Chavarro, Colombia/ Esteban Valdés Arzate, Mexico/ Akwasi Aidoo, Ghana and USA/ Yolanda Pantin, Venezuela/ Yiorgos Chouliaras, Greece/ James O'hara, Mexico, USA

and Ireland/ Raquel Chalfi, Israel/ Jim Byron, USA/
Luisa Vicioso Sánchez, Dominican Republic/ Andrea
Garbin, Italy/ Luz Helena Cordero Villamizar, Colombia/
Peter Voelker, Germany/ Zoran Anchevski, Macedonia/
Naotaka Uematsu, Japan/ Paul Disnard, Colombia/
Vyacheslav Kupriyanov, Russia/ Gabriel Rosenstock,
Ireland/ Maruja Vieira, Colombia/ Nyein Way, Myanmar/
Gaston Bellemare, Québec/ Zohra Hamid, South Africa/
Amir Or, Israel/ Ivan Djeparoski, Macedonia/ Attila F.
Balázs, Slovakia/ Ioana Trica, Romania/ Michaël Glück,
France/ Quito Nicolaas, The Netherlands/ Noria Adel,
Algeria/ Francisco Sánchez Jiménez, Colombia/
Werewere Liking, Cameroon and Ivory Coast/ Beppe
Costa, Italy/ William Pérez Vega, Puerto Rico/ Fanny
Moreno, Colombia/ John Curl, USA/ Kevin Kiely,
Ireland/ Azam Abidov, Uzbekistan/ Luis Galar (No
Country)/ Santiago B. Villafania, Philippines/ Althea
Romeo-Mark, Antigua/ Bengt Berg, Sweden/ Luz
Lescure, Panama/ Lola Koundakjian, Armenia/ Zindzi
Mandela, South Africa/ Edvino Ugolini, Italy/ Jean-
Claude Awono, Cameroon/ Stefania Battistella, Italy/
Eugenia Sánchez Nieto, Colombia/ Alina Beatrice
Chesca, Romania/ Simón Zavala Guzmán, Ecuador/
Ostap Nozhak, Ukraine/ Berry Heart, Botswana/ Gilma
De Los Ríos, Colombia/ Laura Hernandez Muñoz,
México/ Mamang Dai, India/ Erkut Tokman, Turkey/
Álvaro Miranda, Colombia/ Claus Ankersen, Denmark/
Mark Lipman, USA/ John Hegley, England/ Micere
Githae Mugo, Kenya/ Germain Droogenbroodt, Belgium
and Spain/ Fiyinfoluwa Onarinde, Nigeria/ Ataol
Behramoğlu, Turkey/ Khal Torabully, Mauritius and
France/ Jorge Boccanera, Argentina/ Kamanda Kama
Sywor, Congo/ Bineesh Puthuppanam, India/ Iris

Miranda, Puerto Rico/ Pamela Ateka, Kenya/ Fahredin Shehu, Kosovo/ Tamer Öncul, Cyprus/ Tânia Tomé, Mozambique/ Howard A. Fergus, Montserrat, West Indies/ Janak Sapkota, Nepal/ Károly Fellinger, Hungary/ Alfred Tembo, Zambia/ Emilce Strucchi, Argentina/ Juan Diego Tamayo, Colombia/ Manuel Silva Acevedo, Chile/ Elias Letelier, Chile/ Mohammed Bennis, Morocco / Károly Sándor Pallai, Hungary/ Edgardo Nieves-Mieles, Puerto Rico/ Fatoumata Ba, Mali/ Vupenyu Otis Zvoushe, Zimbabwe/ Santosh Alex, India/ Silvana Berki, Albania and Finland/ Hussein Habasch, Kurdistan, Syria/ Lucy Cristina Chau, Panamá/ Jessie Kleemann, Greenland/ Siki Dlanga, South Africa/ Irena Matijašević, Croatia/ Boel Schenlaer, Sweden/ Merlie M. Alunan, Philippines/ Ernesto P. Santiago, Philippines/ Rassool Snyman, South Africa/ Mary Smith, Scotland/ K. Satchidanandan, India/ Sukrita Paul Kumar, India/ Birgitta Jónsdóttir, Iceland/ Zelma White, Montserrat, BWI/ Navkirat Sodhi, India/ Gémino H. Abad, Philippines/ Mbizo Chirasha, Zimbabwe/ Joyce Ashuntantang, Cameroon and USA

Full Page Publishing

ISBN: 978-0-9837708-2-4

www.ingramcontent.com/pod-product-compliance
Lightning Source LLC
Chambersburg PA
CBHW052029290426
44112CB00014B/2446